HAL LEONARD

GUITAR METHOD

Supplement to Any Guitar Method

BARRE CHORDS

TATNALL

To access audio visit:
www.halleonard.com/mylibrary

Enter Code
7617-5105-8824-5119

Recorded at Tatscan Music by Kirk Tatnall
www.kirktatnall.com

ISBN 978-1-4234-7528-6

7777 W. BLUEMOUND RD. P.O. BOX 13819 MILWAUKEE, WI 53213

Visit Hal Leonard Online at
www.halleonard.com

CONTENTS

INTRODUCTION

Welcome to the *Hal Leonard Barre Chords Method*. This book is designed not only as a supplement to the *Hal Leonard Guitar Method* but also to stand on its own by teaching the basic techniques necessary to learn barre chords. As you begin working through this book, you'll immediately notice what sets this method apart: we use real songs!

The arrangements in this book are not note-for-note transcriptions, but they are designed to sound close to the original song while providing an exciting vehicle for learning. Before tackling every nuance of each of these songs, you will need to be able to play and shift between the chords. Upon mastering the chords and techniques used in the arrangements, you will have this first step conquered and ready!

WHAT IS A BARRE CHORD?

Barre chords by definition are "chords in which two or more strings are depressed using the same finger." The fingering shapes can be shifted up or down the neck to different positions to produce other chords of the same quality, making them extremely useful and a staple in many songs across all musical genres. This book will focus on the two most-used groups of barre chords—*sixth-string-root* and *fifth-string-root shapes*—while learning a few others along the way. The goal of this book is for you to completely master the six basic chord forms and develop the ability to switch between them seamlessly.

WHERE DO CHORDS COME FROM?

Before we get into the actual exercises, it is important to develop a knowledge of how chords are built and why certain chords get used with each other. The answer begins with the *major scale*, which is the source from which the vast majority of popular music is created.

Most people will easily recognize the major scale upon hearing a melody sung as, "DO, RE, ME, FA, SOL, LA, TI, and DO." The sound of a scale is defined by its *interval pattern*, or the distances between the notes. These distances are measured with *half steps* (H) and *whole steps* (W). Let's examine the C major scale below. Try playing it up and down a few times to familiarize yourself with its sound. Notice the pattern of half and whole steps and how each note of the scale is given an interval number to identify it.

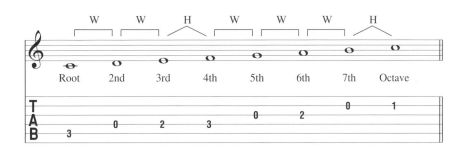

The most basic chord is called a *triad*. Triads consist of three notes and are the basis for the majority of chords in this book. To build a triad from the C scale, we will start with the *root* (first note of the given scale) and add the 3rd and 5th degrees. This is called *stacking 3rds*, obtaining the name from that fact that you start on a note and go up three scale steps to reach the next one. This has also been referred to as "3rd intervals." To make a C triad, we have the notes C–E–G (root–3rd–5th).

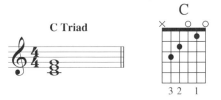

In the key of C, this is known as the *I chord*, since it is built off the first note of the scale. You may notice that the C chord in the grid above has five notes, while our C triad has three. As with many guitar chords, some of the pitches are doubled in different octaves to facilitate strumming and provide a fuller sound. All the notes in the C chord, from lowest to highest, are C–E–G–C–E, and it only uses the notes C, E, and G.

Since there are seven notes in the C major scale, it is possible to stack 3rds off each one of them. Doing so provides a group of chords that all stem directly from the family of C major. This is why a song would be considered in the key of C. Let's build the chord from the second note of the scale by starting on D and stacking 3rds, adding F and A.

Due to the nature of the guitar and its layout, it is not always possible to play the notes in the same order as the triad on the staff, so, as with the C chord, there are extra notes. However, upon studying this chord, you will find that the notes are still D, F, and A.

Since a D major scale normally has an F♯ as the third note, this chord that we built from the second note of C major would be considered to have a *lowered 3rd*, or ♭3rd. Any chord that contains a ♭3rd is called a *minor chord* and is notated by putting a lowercase "m" after the name. Throughout this book, we will be dealing mainly with *major chords* (root–3rd–5th) and minor chords (root–♭3rd–5th). To make a broad generalization, major chords sound happy, while minor chords sound sad.

When labeling chords, Roman numerals are often used to label the note of the scale from which the chord is built. Uppercase Roman numerals are used for major chords, and lowercase are used for minor chords. Since our chord is built from the second note of the C scale, Dm would be referred to as the "iim of C."

Now that we have the basic concept together, let's expand the idea to build the remaining chords in the key of C by stacking 3rds off each individual note. Shown below are the open chords for the key of C major. Go ahead and try them to hear the sound of the harmonized major scale. Don't fret if they are difficult now. The process of mastering them will be broken down throughout the course of this book. Also note that the vii° chord (known as a *diminished* triad: root, ♭3rd, and ♭5th) is not used at all in this book, since it is not often used in most pop songs. It is included here, though, to complete the concept of harmonizing the major scale.

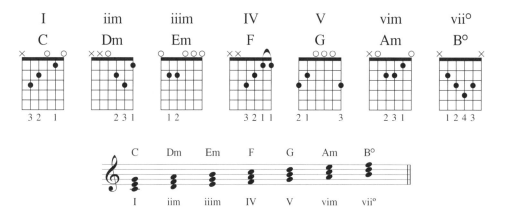

Since each major scale is constructed using the same interval pattern (W–W–H–W–W–W–H), the scales will harmonize in the same order each time. Notice how the pattern remains consistent throughout the five keys listed below. Through repetition and looking at songs from this angle, this pattern will become second nature and provide you with a better understanding of how songs work.

I–iim–iiim–IV–V–vim–vii°

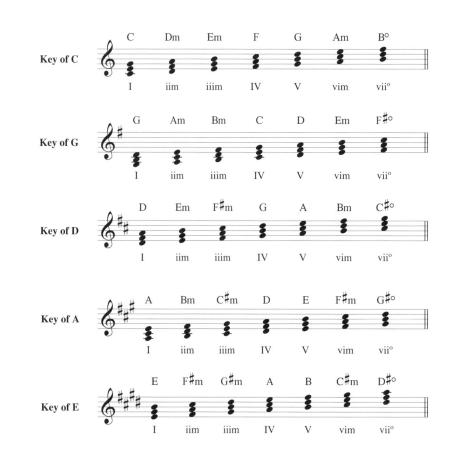

Although not every song works this way, a large amount of songs use a melody created from the major scale and a chord progression that uses its corresponding chords.

SIXTH-STRING-ROOT CHORDS

Throughout the course of learning to play the guitar, every student eventually runs into a chord that is inconvenient or even impossible to play in open position. By mastering the six basic barre chord forms and developing the ability to move them along the neck, you will be prepared for many of the chord changes you will encounter.

Most barre chords originate from modifying an open chord form. In fact, any open chord can be converted into a barre chord by finding a fingering to replace the open strings with fretted notes. By far, the most popular variety of these chords stem from open E chord shapes. Let's begin by reviewing the three basic E chords.

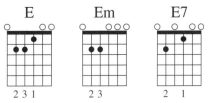

In the case of the open E chord, notice that strings 6, 2, and 1 are left open. To free up a finger to cover them, let's begin by refingering the E chord as shown below:

Now we are ready to turn this into a moveable chord form. We'll start by shifting the entire fingering up one fret. Notice how your first finger is now available to cover the notes that are open strings.

To complete the chord, add your first finger across the first fret, forming a barre where the open strings once were. Notice the similarity between this form and the open E chord. A *curved line* connecting the notes played by the same finger is used to indicate the barre.

While this chord is very challenging at first, practicing the correct positioning of your first finger will help you fret all of the notes properly. Strum all six strings to play your first barre chord then pick each string separately to test for clarity. Here are some tips that will help you get each note ringing clearly:

1. Rather than holding your first finger completely flat, rotate it a little to the side nearest the thumb, allowing the pressure to come slightly from the side of your finger.
2. Position your first finger as close to the fret as possible while still remaining behind it. You may not actually see much of the fret at all. As a general rule, always keep each of your fingers as close to the fret as you can, as it takes less pressure to sound the note clearly.
3. Move the elbow of your fretting hand close to your body, even to the point that it's touching your waist. This will greatly help with the first two steps.
4. Place your thumb directly behind the first-finger barre for additional support. Also, make sure it is positioned low, vertically speaking, allowing your wrist to bend towards you. Moving your thumb higher on the back of the neck makes it difficult to flatten your first finger. Experiment with what works best for you.
5. Try them on an electric guitar. If you don't own one, you don't have to go buy one, but these chords are easier at first on electric. In general, the lighter the gauge and the closer the strings are to the fretboard, the easier they are to press down.

The chord we have just learned is called "F major." Its name comes from the fact that its root note is located under your first finger on string 6—hence, "sixth-string-root chord." This note is used to line the chord up as we move it up and down the neck. Study the diagram of the guitar neck below, taking note of the location of all the natural notes along the sixth string. Play them with your first finger while saying their names aloud.

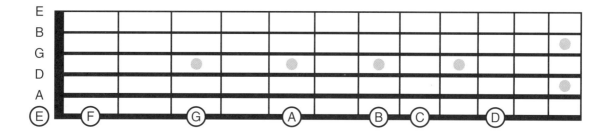

Now we're going to take the chord we learned and move it up and down the neck in the following exercise. If you're struggling with the barre, that's normal. Keep at it, applying all the tips from the previous page. While you are working on that task, you can still play this exercise using the essential bottom four notes of the chord, as shown below. Also, to help with smooth switching, release pressure on beat 3 to allow you to prepare for the next chord change.

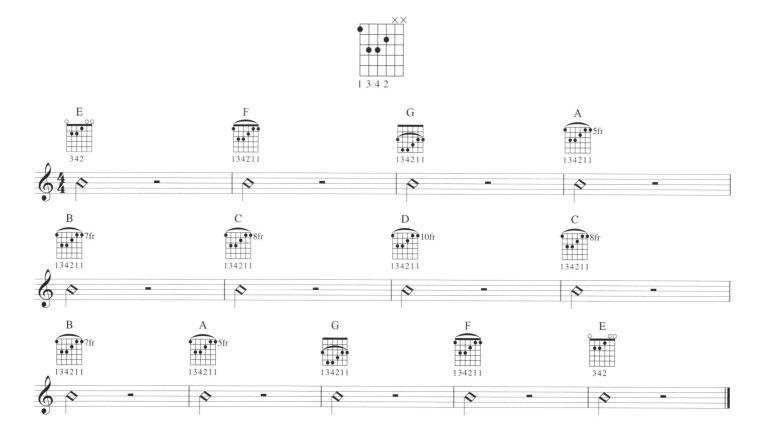

Our next step is to apply the same idea of replacing the open strings to the Em chord. We'll begin by going back to the open position and modifying the chord form. Take the standard Em fingering and change it to accommodate barring the open strings.

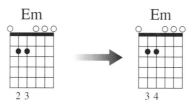

Using fingers 3 and 4 will allow you to cover the open strings with a barre. Slide them up one fret and lay your first finger across the first fret to complete the Fm chord. Since this form has an extra note to barre, it can present some new challenges. Strum the chord, then play each note separately to determine if each note is sounding clearly, and apply all the tips from when we learned the F chord. Notice how, in the picture, the second finger is reinforcing the first. This can help to apply the pressure needed for the barre. Keep your third and fourth fingers arched and on their tips to ensure the third string is not muted.

In the following exercise, we will move this form up and down the neck. Remember that the root is under your first finger on string 6. Look at the neck diagram to determine on which fret to play the chord. This will help you learn where the notes are along string 6, which is essential for applying these chord shapes.

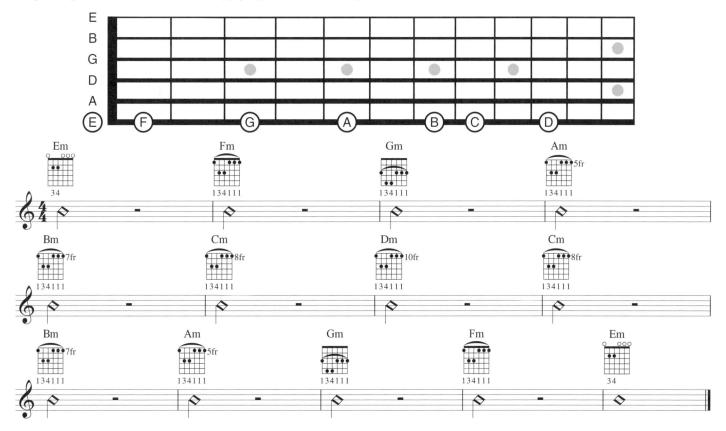

Finally, let's use this same concept to modify our third chord form on string 6: the *dominant seventh*. Exchange fingers 2 and 1 for fingers 3 and 2, once again freeing your first finger for barring.

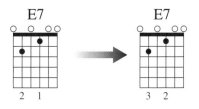

Slide fingers 3 and 2 up a fret and complete the chord by barring across fret 1 with your first finger. Now we have a moveable seventh chord form. You may notice that this is similar to the major form with the exception that there is no fourth finger. The big challenge with this chord form is staying on your fingertips with your second and third fingers, allowing strings 2 and 4 to ring freely. Be sure to arch your fingers and not lock your knuckles.

As with the previous chords, our root note is under our first finger on string 6. Move the chord along the neck in this next exercise, referencing the neck diagram when needed. We're not only practicing our seventh chord form, but we're also learning all the natural notes along string 6.

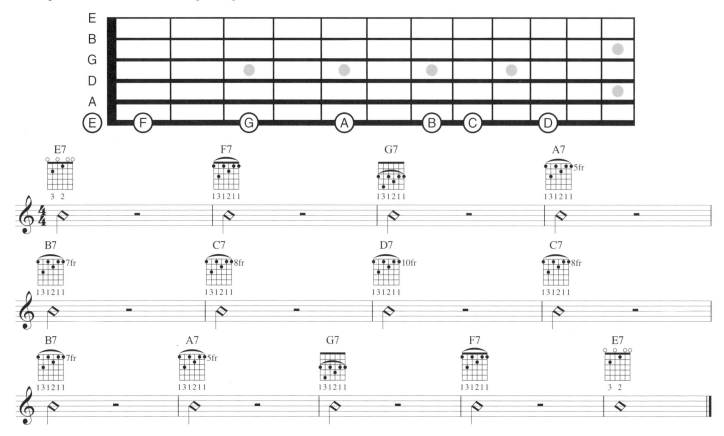

Now that you have learned the three basic sixth-string-root chord forms, it is time to put them to work in some real-life situations. In addition to having three chords that can be easily moved around the neck to fit any chord you may need, barre chords offer another unique asset: easily muted strumming. A *muted strum* is a percussive effect that is used to give your strum patterns a rhythmic boost. To perform this technique, simply release the pressure from the barre chord so all your fingers are still touching the strings but not the guitar neck; keep your fingers positioned in the barre chord form, as well. The resulting sound should be that of a percussive "chick" in which no notes are sounded at all. If you are hearing a note, check your fretting hand and make sure you are not pressing the strings down all the way to the frets.

When notating a muted strum, an "X" is placed on the staff rather than a chord slash. One of the most popular ways to use a muted strum is to place it on beats 2 and 4. This accents the *back beat*, much like a drummer does with the snare drum. It is particularly useful when there is no drummer and you need to help the rhythm along. Let's get the feel for this by trying it on one chord. Keep your picking hand swinging like a pendulum, strumming down on the beats and up on the "&s." Release the pressure on beats 2 and 4 and accent the strum with your picking hand. If you need help finding the root of the chord, consult the neck diagram above.

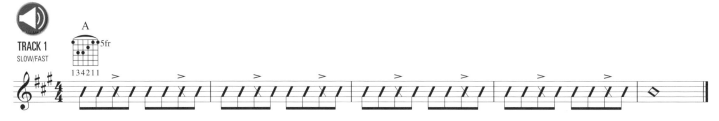

Try this technique with these popular strum patterns. Remember, you should not hear any actual pitches during the muted strum.

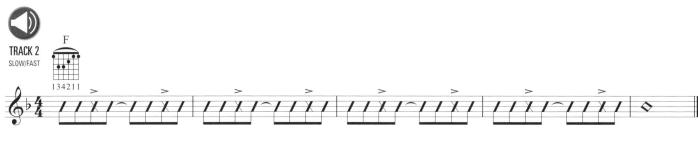

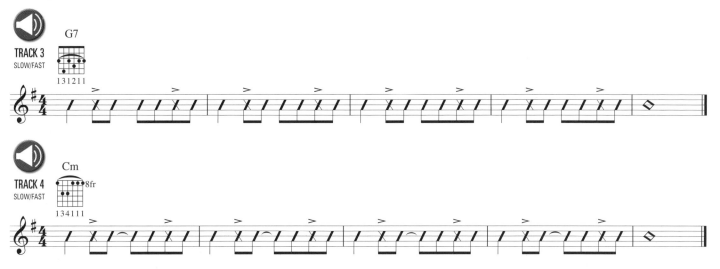

Another important part of the muting technique occurs when switching between barre chords. In many situations, a muted strum is needed to get from one chord to another, especially when moving large distances along the neck. These often occur naturally on the "&" (upstroke) of beat 4, since it is of utmost importance to squarely complete the chord change on beat 1. Most guitarists do this almost subconsciously, so it is rarely discussed. Shining a light on this technique will help you sound like a pro.

In the following exercises, the goal is to keep your picking hand on autopilot—always strumming down on the beats and up on the "&s." As you switch between chords, release the pressure of your fretting hand while starting to move on the "&" of beat 4. This will produce the muted strum as notated, allowing you to cleanly make the chord change on beat 1, which is absolutely the most-important factor in sounding good.

Remember to keep the tempo slow at first, concentrating on playing the exercises correctly. Increase the tempo only after you can cleanly make the changes. Again, reference the neck diagram if you have trouble finding the roots of these chords.

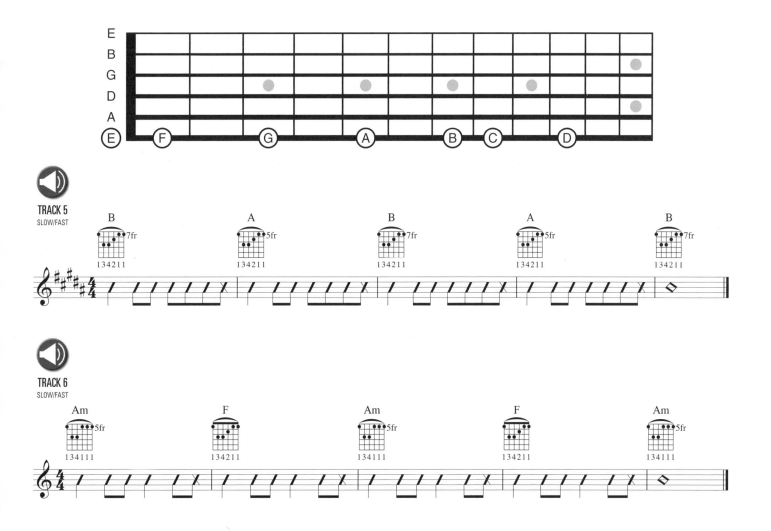

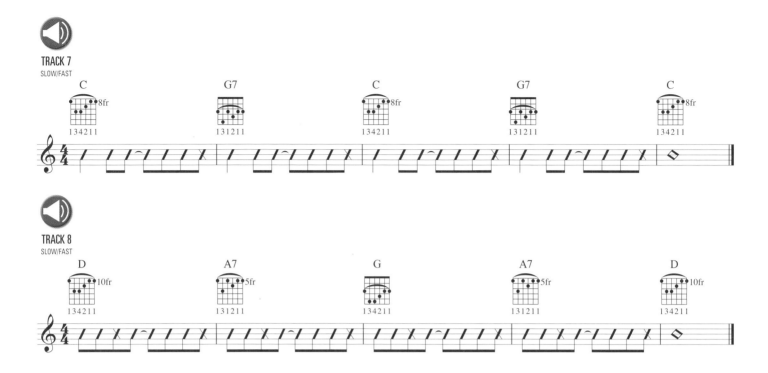

MAJOR SIXTH-STRING-ROOT CHORD EXERCISES

The goal of the following exercises is to help you get familiar with moving the three sixth-string-root chords along the neck. Practice each exercise slowly at first and be aware of the muted strums that allow you to easily switch from chord to chord.

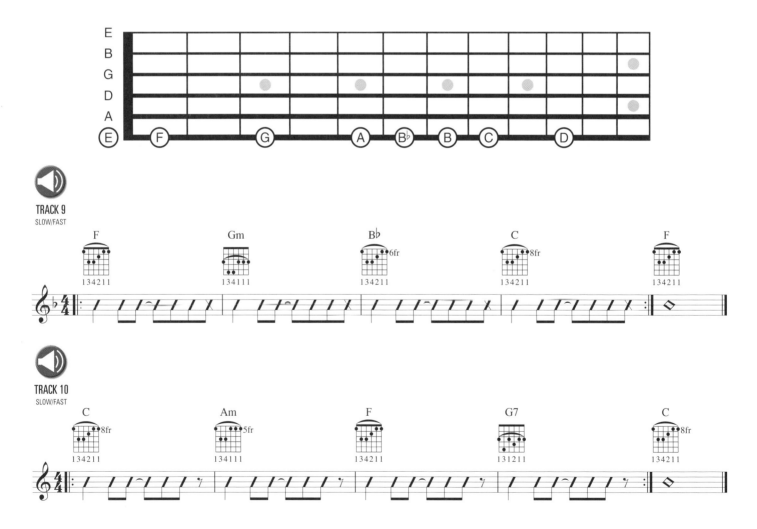

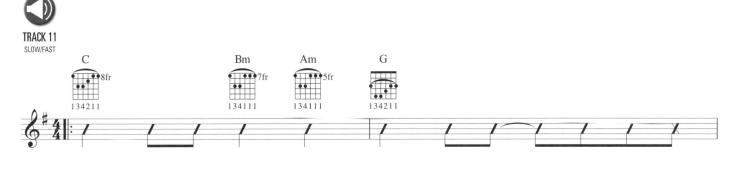

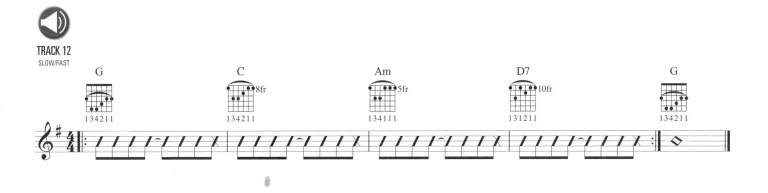

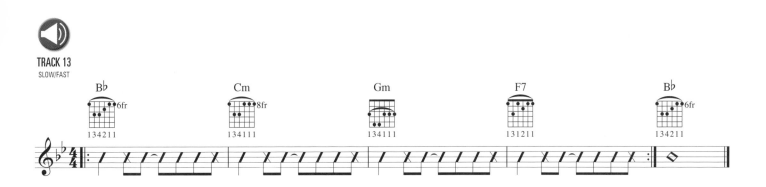

MINOR SIXTH-STRING-ROOT CHORD EXERCISES

Like the previous page, these exercises consist of some common chord movements that you will encounter when learning songs. These are based around minor keys. Take your time and concentrate on accuracy before speed.

"All Along the Watchtower" — Jimi Hendrix

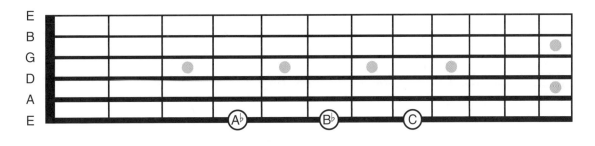

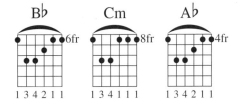

Now it's time to put our new chord shapes to work in some real songs. To master this classic, let's break the riff down and focus on the rhythm while simultaneously learning the chord movements. The toughest thing about this one is switching on the "&" of 4. Take it slow and concentrate on the rhythm.

TRACK 19

For the second half of the riff, move the chord down two frets instead of up. The rhythm and strum patterns are the same.

TRACK 20

Finally, we'll combine the movements and add the remaining strums to complete the pattern.

TRACK 21

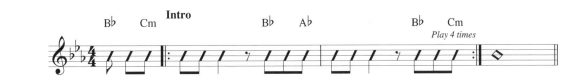

"Stray Cat Strut" – The Stray Cats

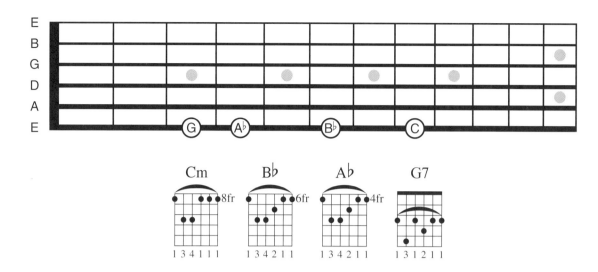

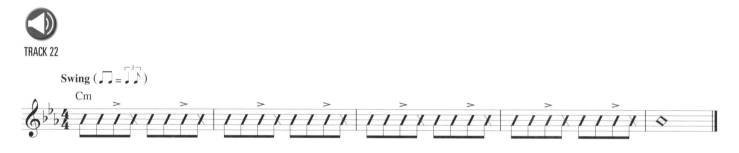

The first thing you may notice about "Stray Cat Strut" is that it adds one new chord to the three we used in the previous song. Before we play the whole tune, let's get a feel for the strum pattern by playing it on one chord. Try accenting beats 2 and 4 to help the swing feel.

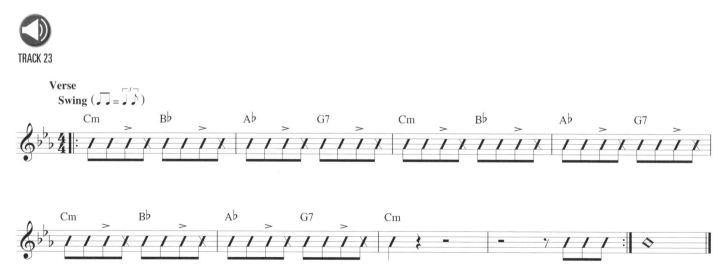

Now take the strum pattern through the chord changes. Make sure you have it smooth and steady before increasing the tempo.

"Creep" — Radiohead

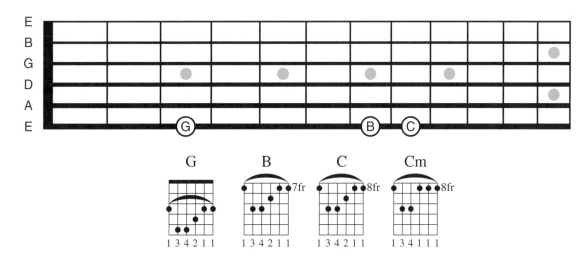

In our next riff, pay attention to the large jump between the G and the B chords. The muted strum will allow you time to make the switch. You may want to perfect the two-measure strum pattern before applying it to the song.

TRACK 24

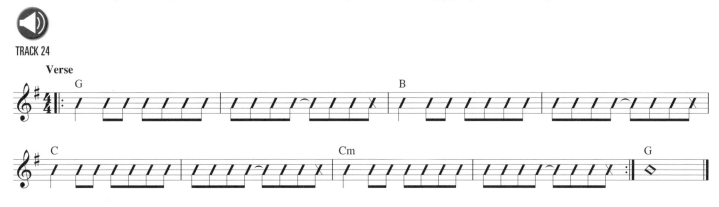

"(Sittin' On) The Dock of the Bay" — Otis Redding

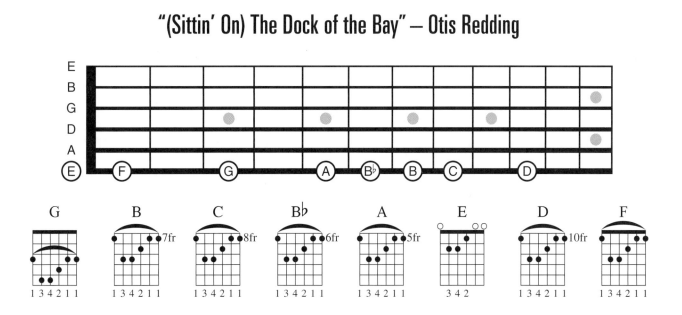

This Otis Redding classic uses only the major barre chord form but covers the length of the neck using it. As with any piece of music, learning can often be made easier by breaking it down into smaller pieces that you can then string together. As you try the first line of the full arrangement on the next page, you will realize the first three chords are the same as the previous song. The difficulty lies in moving the chord while playing solid eighth notes.

As you play the following phrase, temporarily relax your grip as you move the chord.

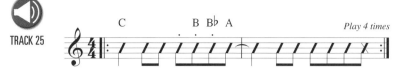

To facilitate smooth switching, remove your first finger and shift the remaining three to the open position for the E chord.

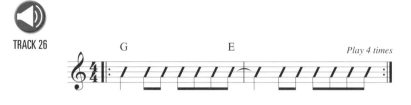

The final two exercises address the long jumps required to play the bridge of the song. Take your time and take advantage of the muted strums to execute the changes.

FIFTH-STRING-ROOT CHORDS

As we learned in Chapter 1, all barre chords originate from modifying the fingering of an open chord form, allowing the strings that were once open to be fretted. The second most popular variety of barre chords stem from open A chord shapes. Let's review the three basic A chords:

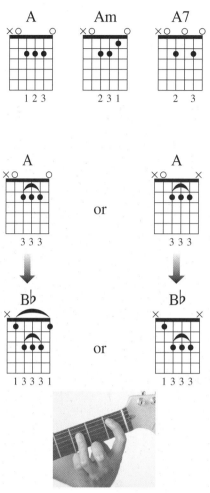

Applying the same concepts as Chapter 1, let's figure out a way to convert the open A chord into a moveable chord form. Notice that the A chord has three notes on the second fret. We will begin the process by creating a barre across these notes with our third finger. Keep your finger close to the second fret and lock the knuckle that is closest to your fingertip; this will elevate your middle knuckle, allowing the open first string to ring. This note, however, is not essential to the chord. In fact, many people can't bend their knuckle this far. In this case, let your third finger lightly touch string 1, muting it out. The trick is to fret the second string but not the first; tilting your fretting hand slightly towards the nut may aid in this process.

Now we are ready to slide this chord up one fret and add our first finger where the open strings once were. Keep your wrist bent and your thumb in the middle or lower region of the neck.

As is the case with sixth-string-root chords, the name of our new moveable chord form comes from the fact that the root note is located under your first finger on string 5. Study the diagram below of all the natural notes on the fifth string, and then play them up and down the neck while saying their names aloud.

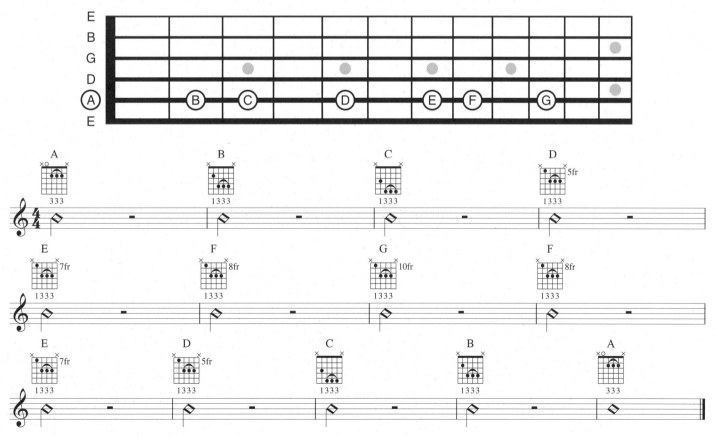

Next, we'll convert the open Am chord to its moveable form. Keeping with our process, rearrange your fingers to fret Am, as shown in the chord frames below:

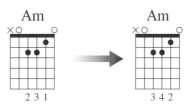

Our first finger is now available to complete the barre. Shift fingers 2, 3, and 4 up a fret and barre strings 1 through 5 with your first finger. You may notice that this new form is identical to the major form on string 6 but shifted up a set of strings—all the same fingering advice applies. Make sure your fingers are arched and on their tips, allowing the adjacent strings to sound clear.

Let's take our new minor chord form and move it along the fifth string. The individual chord frames are removed again to reinforce learning the location of the natural notes; use the neck diagram to locate the roots. You may want to try this with your first finger only prior to moving the entire chord.

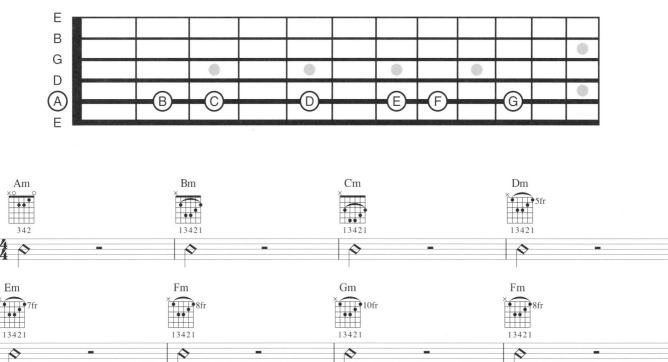

Finally, we'll apply the open chord-conversion process to our last fifth-string-root chord: the dominant seventh. Switching your fingers to 3 and 4, as shown below, will provide the reach necessary to replace the open strings.

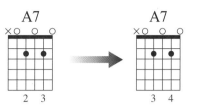

Move the chord up one fret and apply the barre to the first fret, forming our moveable dominant seventh chord form. Like most of our previous fingerings, staying on your fingertips and keeping your fingers arched is essential for successfully fretting this chord. As is the case with the sixth-string minor form, you may consider reinforcing the barre with your second finger.

As in our previous exercises, let's practice our new chord form while learning the notes along string 5. Consult the neck diagram when necessary.

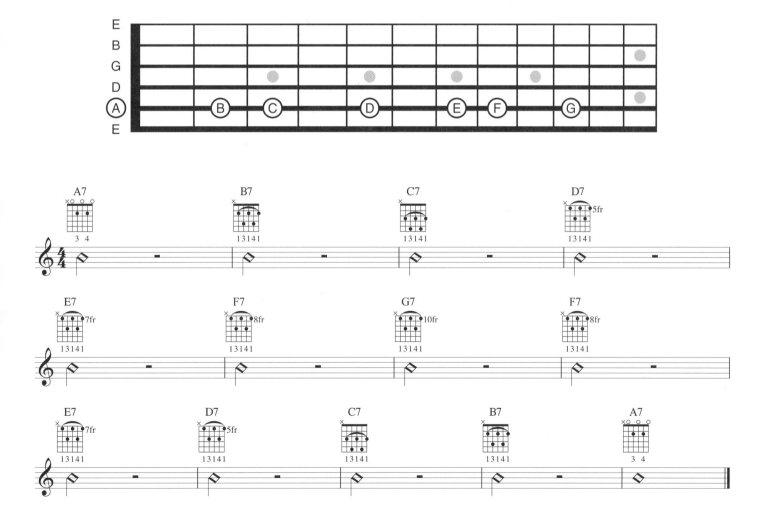

MAJOR FIFTH-STRING-ROOT CHORD EXERCISES

As you practice these exercises, they may feel familiar. The examples are the same as the sixth-string section but transposed to work with our three new chords that utilize string 5.

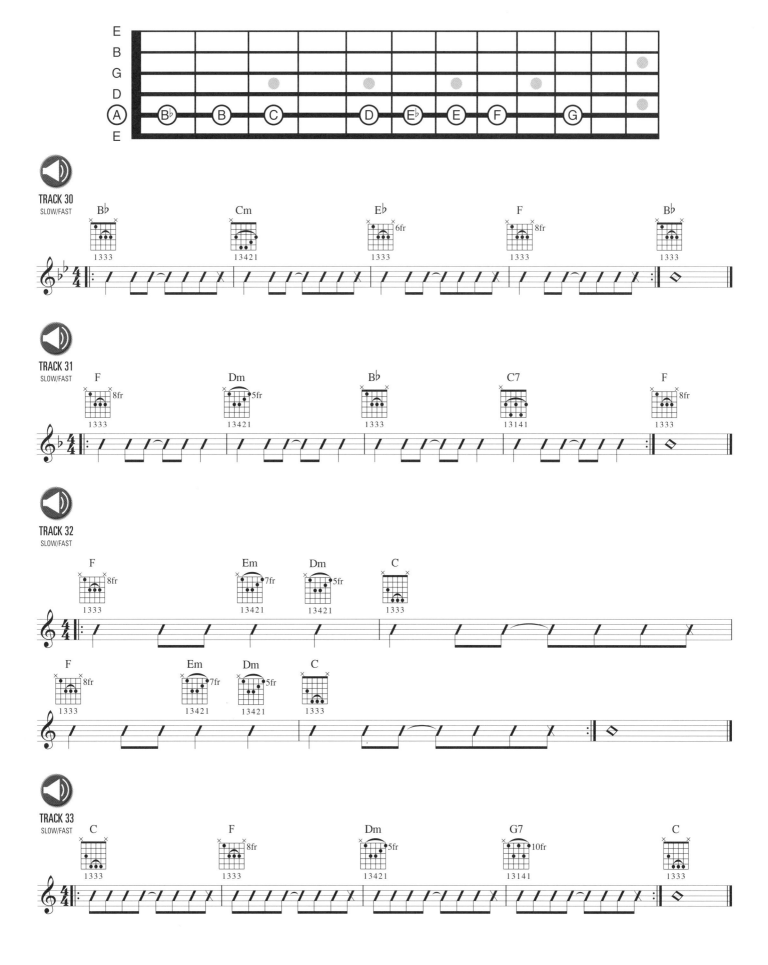

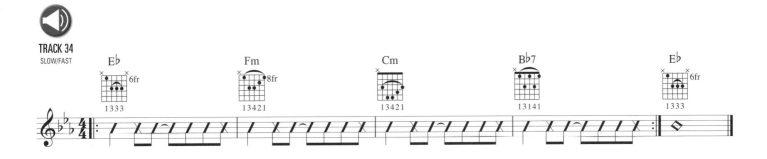

MINOR FIFTH-STRING-ROOT CHORD EXERCISES

Again, these minor examples are transposed versions of the patterns you've already learned on string 6. Notice that the distances between the chords are the same but on string 5.

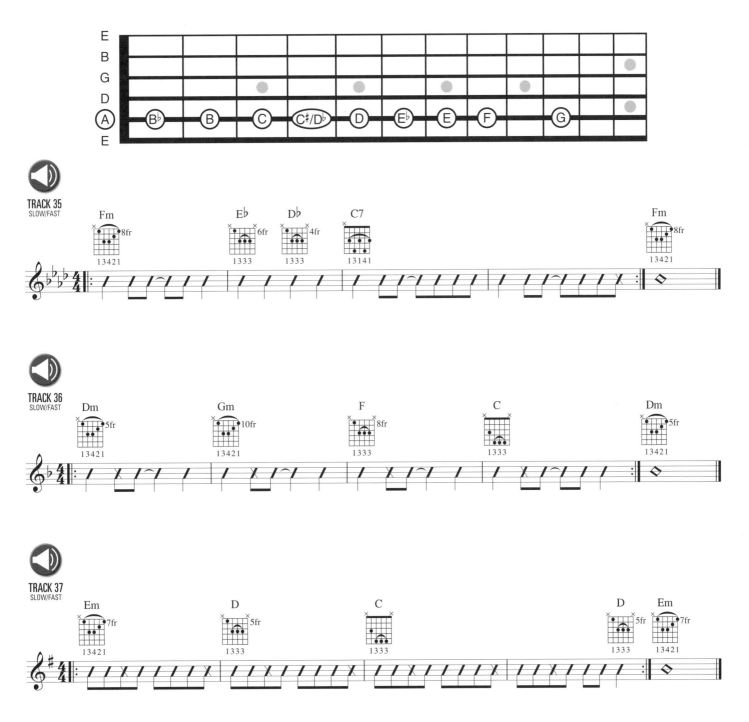

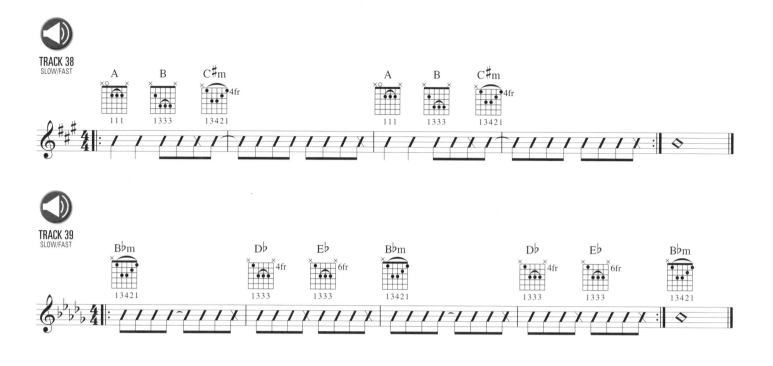

"Stray Cat Strut" – The Stray Cats

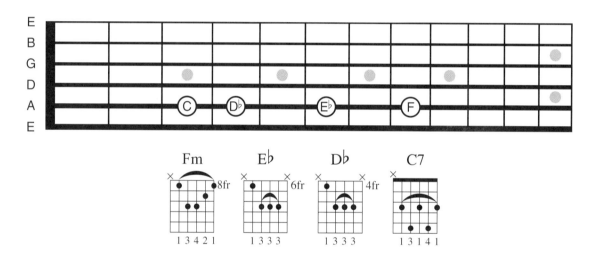

Our first song on string 5 uses all three qualities of our new chords. Notice that the root movements and rhythms from the sixth-string version are identical.

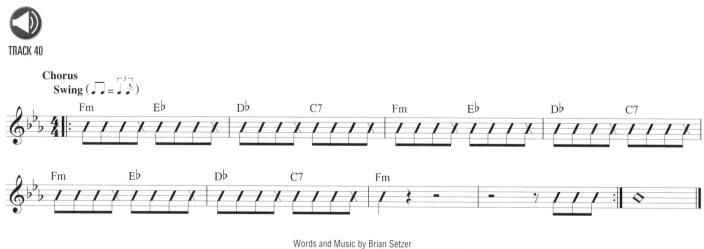

Words and Music by Brian Setzer
© 1981 EMI LONGITUDE MUSIC and ROCKIN' BONES MUSIC
All Rights Controlled and Administered by EMI LONGITUDE MUSIC
All Rights Reserved   International Copyright Secured   Used by Permission

"I Can't Explain" — The Who

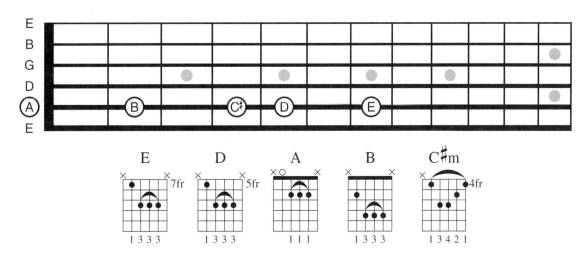

Along with being fun to play, "I Can't Explain" makes for a great chord-switching exercise due to the larger distances between some of the chords. Make sure the first string is muted on the major chord form.

TRACK 41

"American Woman" – The Guess Who

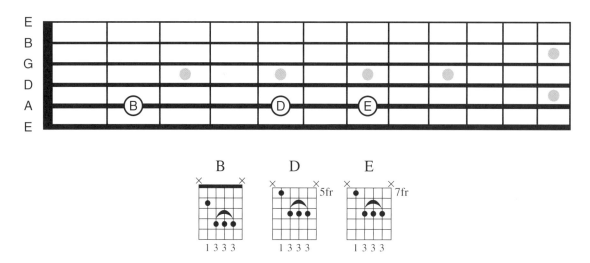

This song only uses one chord form but can still be tricky due to the sixteenth-note strum pattern and the speed at which you need to change chords. To get the chord movements and the strum pattern down, let's first learn the pattern with an eighth-note strum at a slow tempo. Be sure to master the pickstrokes correctly the first time, as they will remain in the same pattern when we switch to sixteenths.

TRACK 42

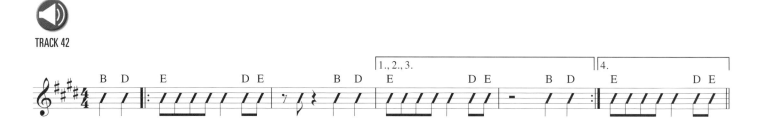

To make the switch to sixteenth notes, mute the strings with your fretting hand and play the following exercise. Notice that, when there are four strums per beat, the numbers and the "&s" become downstrokes. Say the count aloud and tap your foot on the quarter note as you get a feel for the pattern. When you have the rhythm locked in, play the riff below; the strum pattern is the same:

TRACK 43

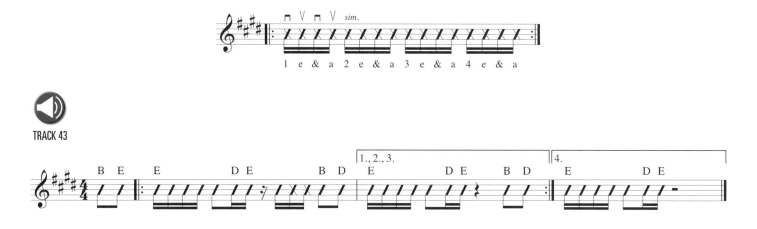

Written by Burton Cummings, Randy Bachman, Gary Peterson and Jim Kale

COMBINING FIFTH- AND SIXTH-STRING-ROOT CHORDS

Now that you've learned the six most-important barre chord forms, it's time to put them to work. More often than not, songs frequently switch between chords with the root on strings 5 and 6. This enables guitarists to play a greater variety of chords without moving large distances along the neck. Before we look at some actual songs, let's examine two of the most popular chord progressions.

A *chord progression* is simply the order or pattern of chords that occur in a song. Most frequently, these patterns are generated by building a chord on each degree of the major scale. To label each of these chords, a Roman numeral that corresponds to the scale degree is used. Our first chord pattern, the I–IV–V, is the most-used progression in Western music. Let's take a look at it in the key of C:

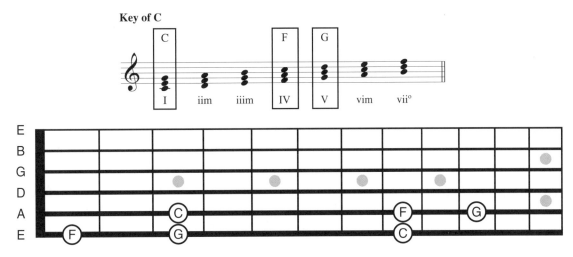

Notice that, when the roots of the chords are placed on the neck diagram, there are two convenient spots where the chords are close to each other: one with the root on string 6, and another with the root on string 5. Both patterns create an "L" shape with two frets between the IV and V chords. Depending on the key of the song and the situation in which it is used, one of these patterns may fit better than the other. As you practice the following exercises, make sure to pay attention to the "L" shape of the root movement as it will occur in many more songs to come. Being able to identify the chord progression will provide a better understanding of a song and aid in learning it.

Using the neck diagram as a guide, play each exercise twice with the root chord (C) on string 5, then twice with the root chord on string 6.

I ON STRINGS 5 & 6

I–IV–V

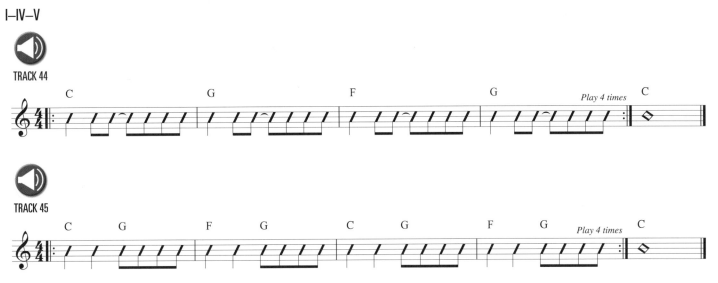

The second chord progression we will examine adds one chord to our first progression, resulting in I, IV, V and vim. These chords have been widely used in many styles of music throughout history. Let's look at four different ways this chord progression is commonly laid out on the guitar neck. Two will have the I chord on string 6, and two will have the I chord on string 5. Once again, observe the pattern of the root movement, as these will recur throughout many songs you learn in the future.

I ON STRING 6

I–vim–IV–V

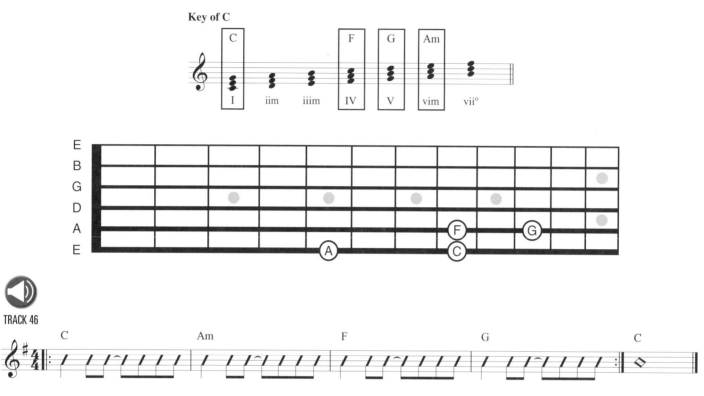

TRACK 46

I–V–vim–IV

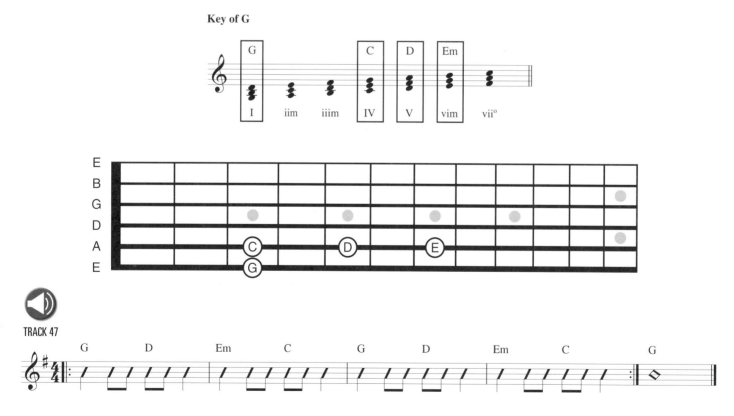

TRACK 47

I ON STRING 5

I–IV–vim–V

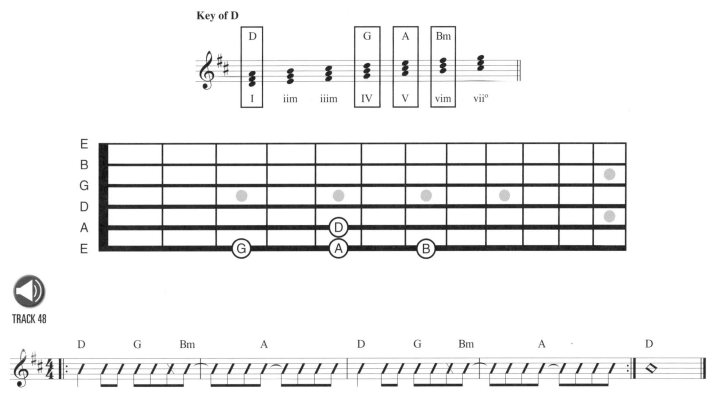

TRACK 48

I–V–vim–IV

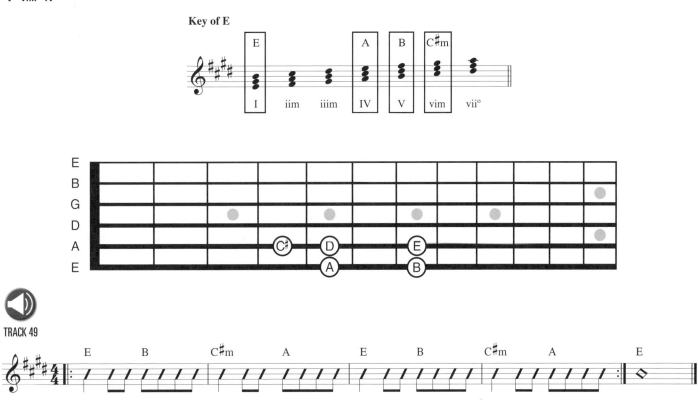

TRACK 49

"Stray Cat Strut" – The Stray Cats

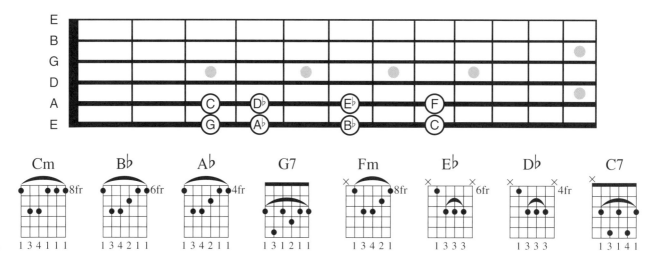

The full arrangement of "Stray Cat Strut" combines the chord patterns we learned in the previous examples. Notice how the root movement and chord qualities remain the same, but the chord shapes needed for each string are different.

TRACK 50

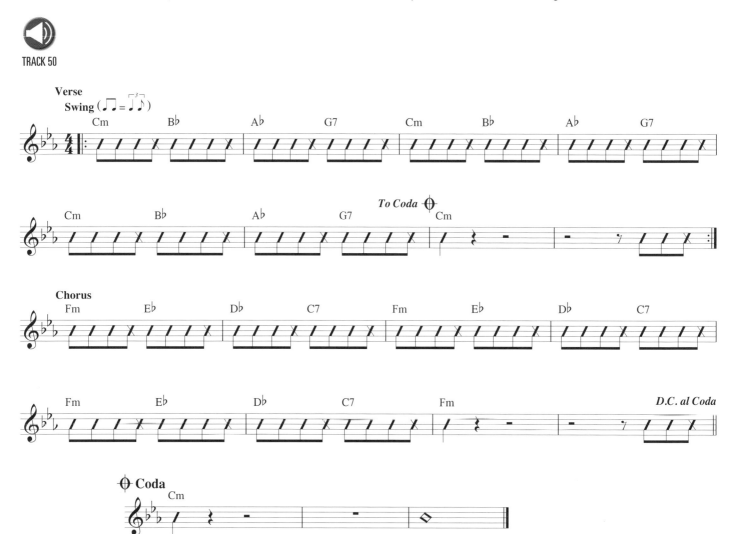

"Jamming'" – Bob Marley

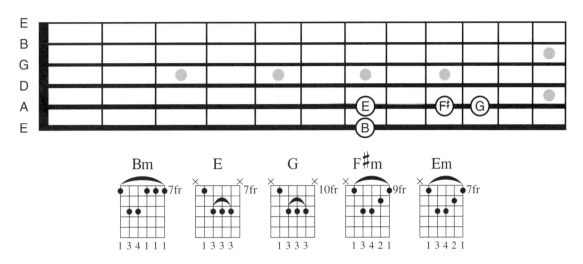

One of the key ingredients of reggae music is that the guitar accents the upbeats, or in the case of "Jamming," beats 2 and 4. Often the guitarist focuses the strumming on the highest notes of the chord. The first line of the arrangement simulates the keyboard part and offers another example of switching chords on the upbeats.

TRACK 51

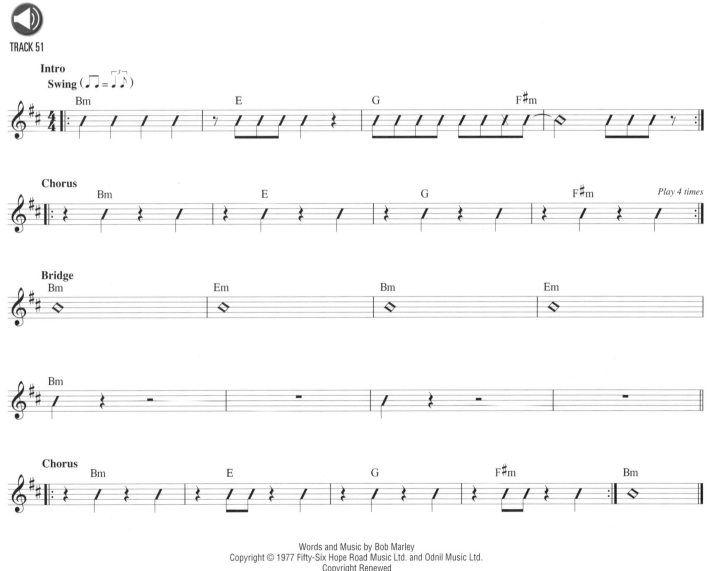

MORE CHORDS AND PATTERNS

This section introduces more chord types, strum patterns, and plenty of great songs!

"She Will Be Loved" — Maroon5

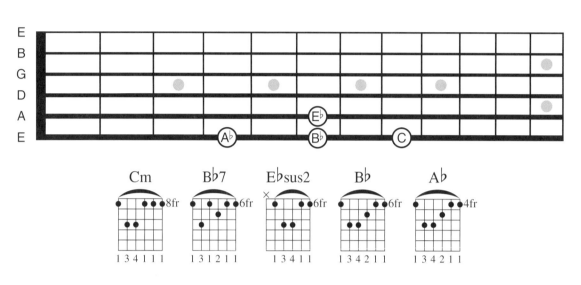

Our new song introduces us to a new variation of the fifth-string-root chord form: the *suspended second* (sus2). Replacing the 3rd of the chord with the 2nd provides an open, ambiguous texture. Notice how the muted strums are used not only to facilitate switching but also to add rhythmic movement to the progression.

TRACK 52

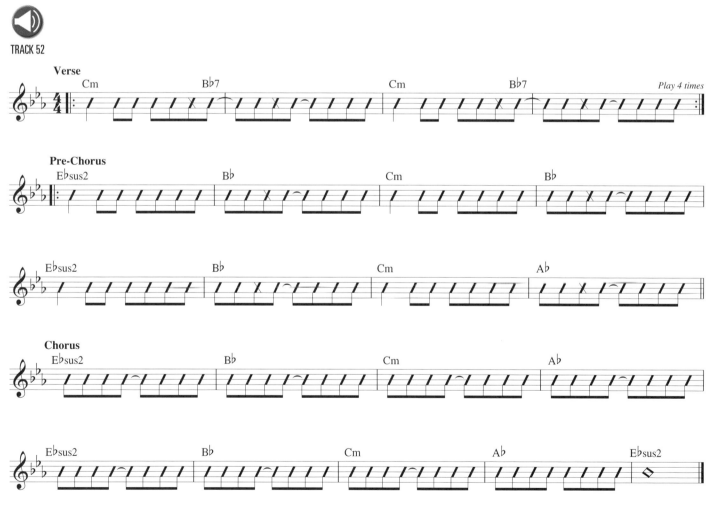

"California Girls" — The Beach Boys

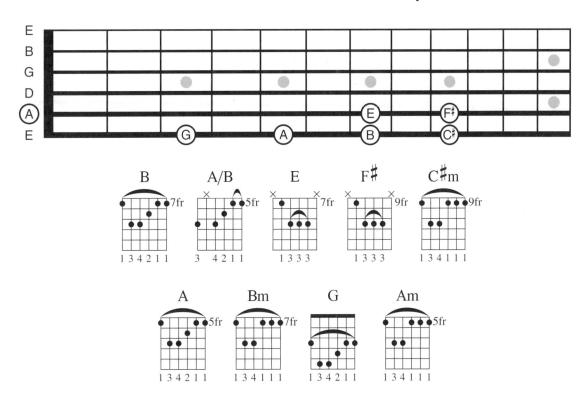

This Beach Boys classic offers a good range of barre chord forms and fairly straightforward strumming patterns. The one new chord, A/B, is a variation of our sixth-string major form known as a *slash chord*. The letter to the right of the slash refers to the lowest note of the chord, telling us that it is an A chord with a B in the bass. Before learning the arrangement, practice switching between the B and A/B chords—notice that fingers 2 and 4 remain consistent. Release the pressure and keep them touching the strings as you shift between chords.

TRACK 53

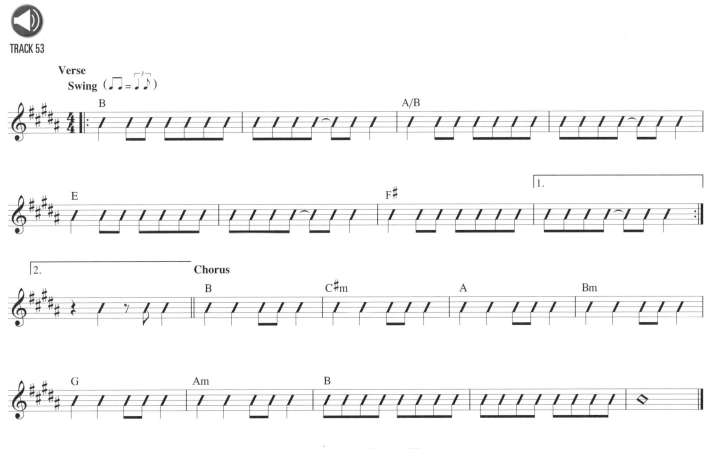

"Just Like Heaven" — The Cure

In looking at this arrangement, you may notice that it uses only one strum pattern. Before trying the tune, play the strum pattern with any chord from the song; this will allow you to get the rhythm going prior to switching the chords. The placement of the muted strums will allow you to make the changes smoothly. Notice the "type 2" D chord at the end of the song. When you see this label, it refers to another voicing of a previously-used chord.

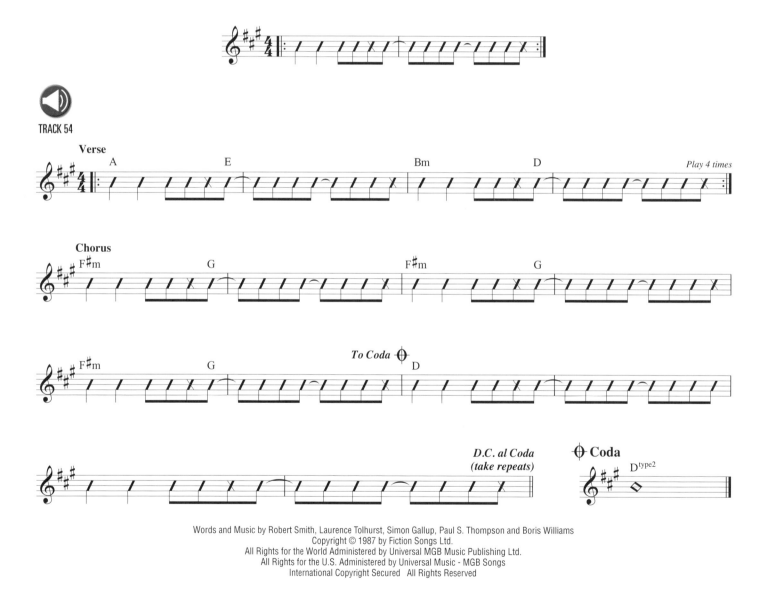

TRACK 54

Words and Music by Robert Smith, Laurence Tolhurst, Simon Gallup, Paul S. Thompson and Boris Williams

"Surrender" — Cheap Trick

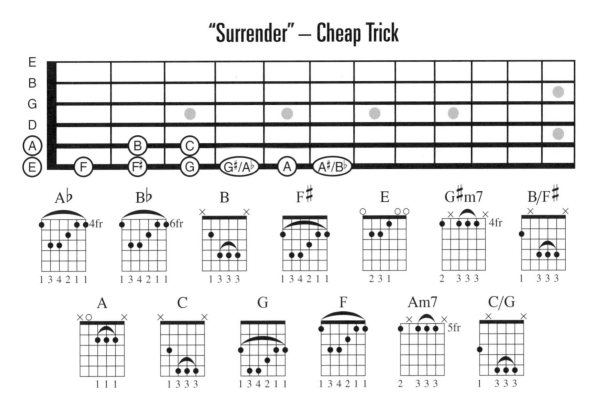

Cheap Trick's 1978 hit "Surrender" is a great example of a song that uses both I–IV–V and I–IV–V–vim chord progressions. In the latter, we are introduced to the idea of moving the bass note only to change the chord. In the Chorus, observe how your third finger remains in place from the B chord and only the lowest note moves. You may recognize the root-movement pattern as the first of the two "I chord on string 5" patterns from earlier in the chapter. Also, take notice of how the root movements of the entire song stay the same but shift up one fret as the key changes from B to C.

TRACK 55

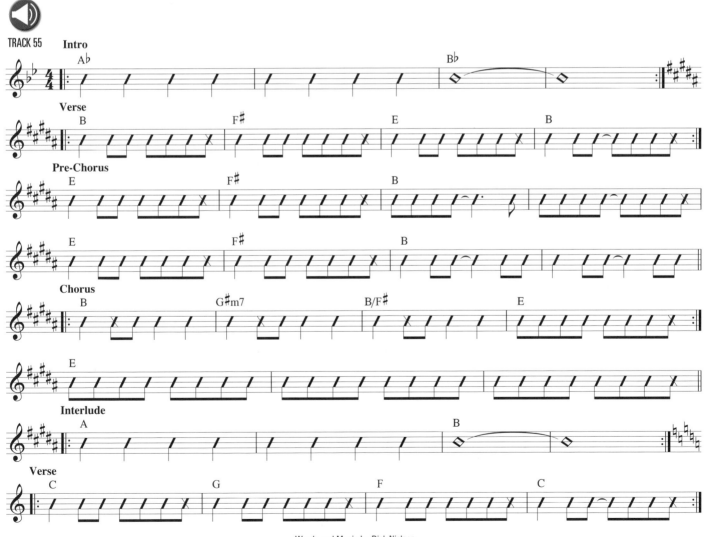

Words and Music by Rick Nielsen

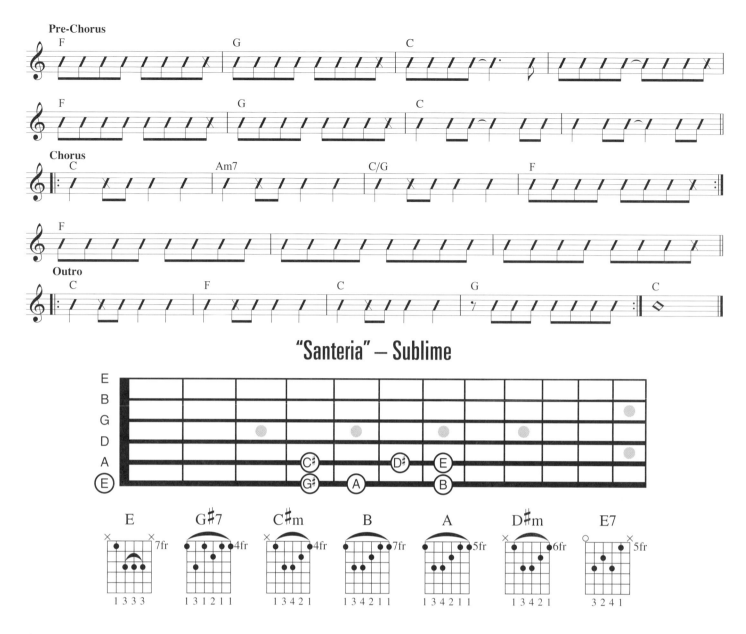

"Santeria" – Sublime

"Santeria" utilizes two main strum patterns: the first one is the familiar reggae strum which accents all of the upbeats, or the "&s." Plot out where the four chords are used before adding the rhythm. The second strum pattern condenses a popular pattern into two beats with sixteenth notes. Try accenting the lowest note of the chord on the chord change. Reference the audio example when necessary. The last chord is a non-barre version of the 5th-string-root E7 chord.

TRACK 56

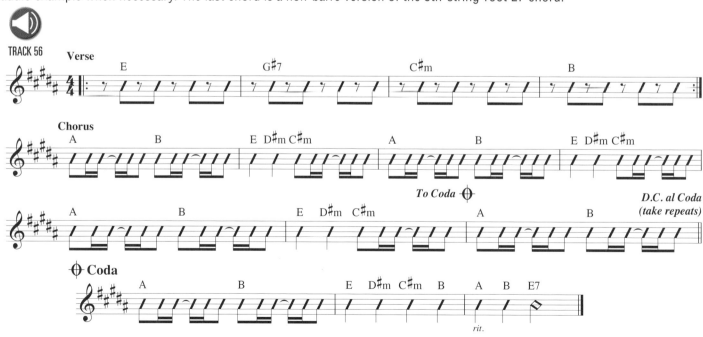

"Layla" (Unplugged Version) — Eric Clapton

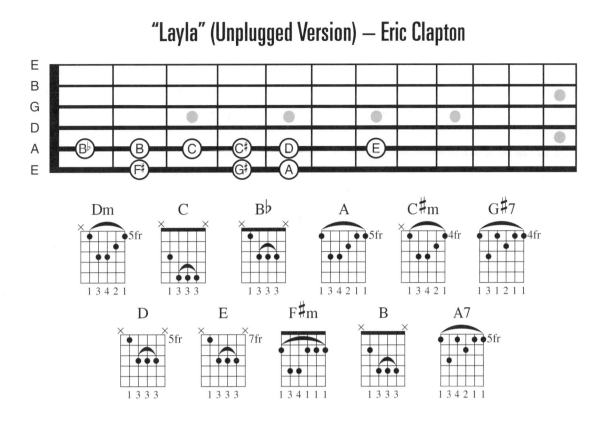

"Layla" makes excellent use of barre chords, partially due to the fact that it crosses through the keys of Dm and E in its relatively short form. The first riff involves switching chords very quickly. You may want to practice it first, concentrating on maintaining the correct strumming pattern while switching chords.

TRACK 57

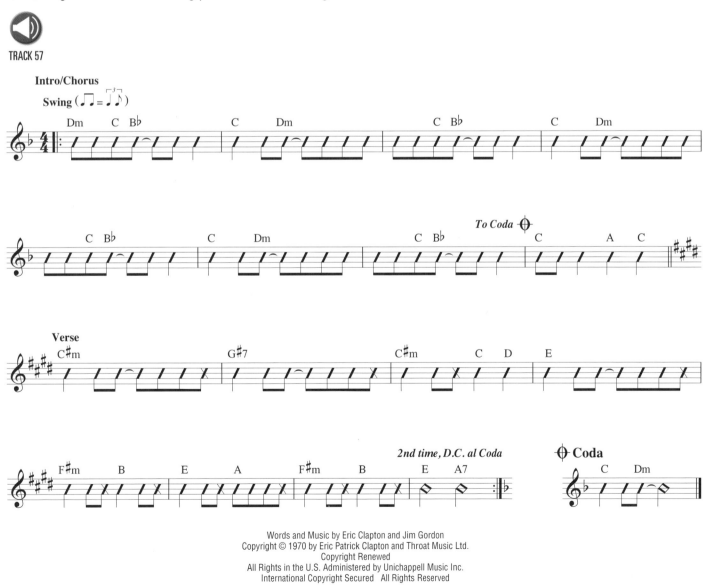

"Suffragette City" – David Bowie

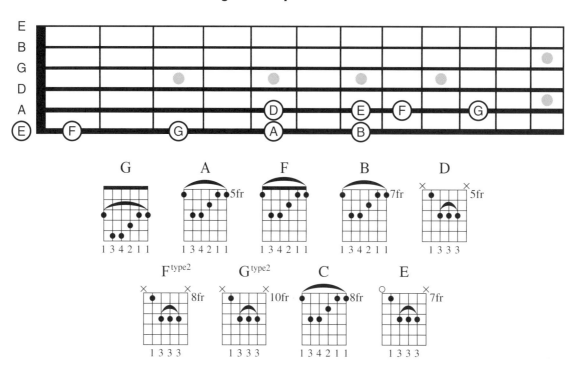

This David Bowie classic introduces a new technique: *sliding*. Before we explore this, let's master the main strumming pattern of the arrangement. Any other strums that occur are variations of this rhythmic feel.

TRACK 58

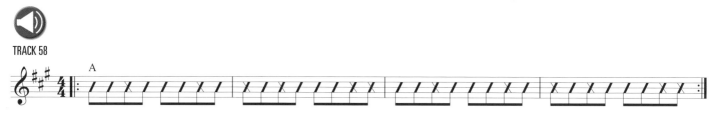

There are two basic ways to slide a barre chord. In our first example, the rhythm slashes between G and A are connected by a diagonal line. This indicates that you keep the pressure applied to the G and slide the entire fingering up to A, striking the A chord on beat 1 when you arrive there.

TRACK 59

The second method uses the actual slide to sound the chord you are sliding into. This is notated by placing a curved line above the diagonal line that indicates the slide. In the following example, use the slide to sound the G chord, and let your pick miss the strings on beat 3 to keep your picking hand on track.

TRACK 60

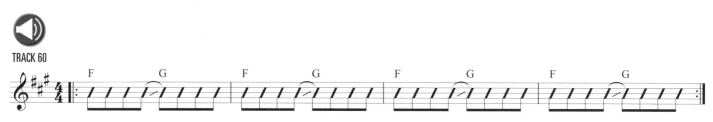

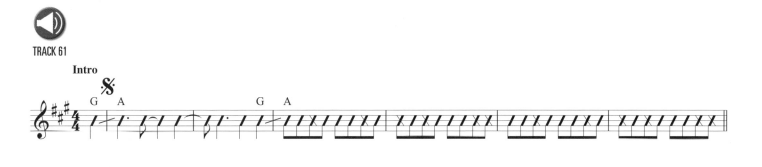

Intro

Verse

Chorus

To Coda

D.S. al Coda (no repeats)

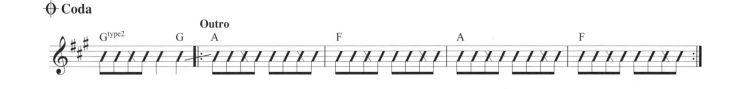

Coda

Outro

"All My Loving" – The Beatles

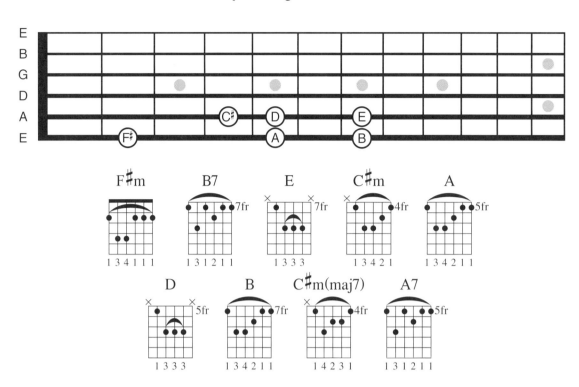

"All My Loving" uses many different chords from the key of E and introduces us to a new minor chord variation: the *minor (major seventh)*. This chord lowers the root in the middle of the chord a half step (one fret) to the seventh of the scale. Practice switching between these chords slowly and smoothly.

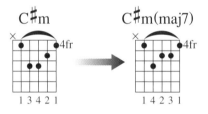

Before playing the arrangement, let's take a minute to master each of the strum patterns used. Play each exercise and focus on getting the timing perfect. Always strum down on the numbers and up on the "&s."

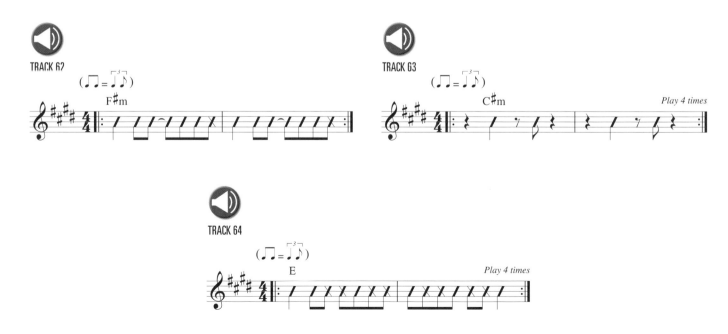

Verse
Swing (♫ = ♩♪)

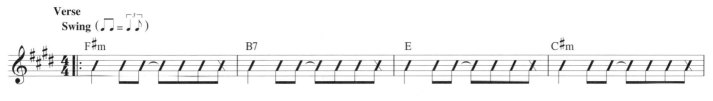

Chorus

To Coda ⊕

Guitar Solo

D.C. al Coda
(no repeats)

⊕ **Coda**   **Outro**

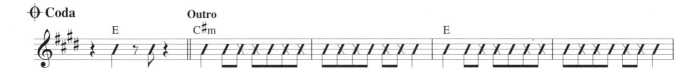

"What It Takes" — Aerosmith

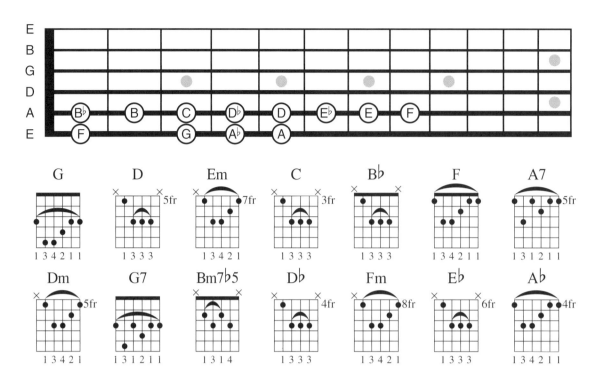

"What It Takes" presents many challenges since it's a long arrangement with many sections, chord changes, and a new barre chord as well (Bm7♭5). Let's begin by looking at the chord progressions. As with any big project, the key is to break it down into smaller pieces and work on them separately so putting them together will be much easier. The next five exercises remove the difficult strumming patterns, allowing us to focus solely on learning the patterns and switching the chords. As you play them, look at the arrangement to spot where they occur in the song.

Our next hurdle to get over is changing chords on the "&" of beats 3 and 4. This occurs twice in the song. Although each example uses different chords, they both start on a minor chord and move down in whole steps (two frets) to major chords. You may recognize this pattern from other songs we've encountered and you'll surely come across it again.

Our final step before playing the song is to work on the three main strumming patterns. Start slow and remember to keep the swing feel as you practice them. Referencing the audio example will help you with the feel.

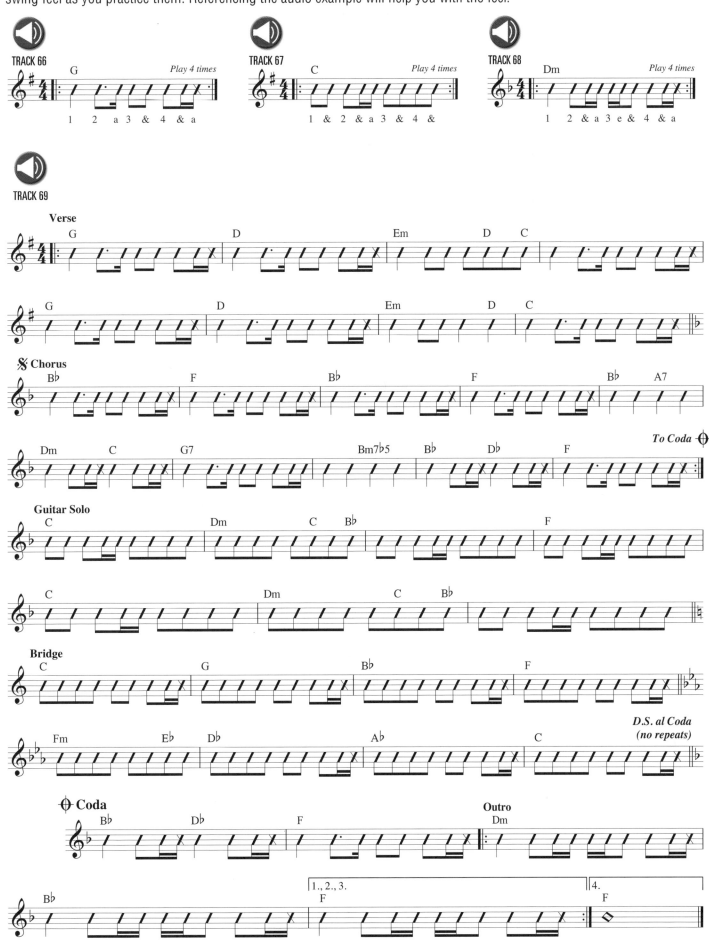

"Hook" — Blues Traveler

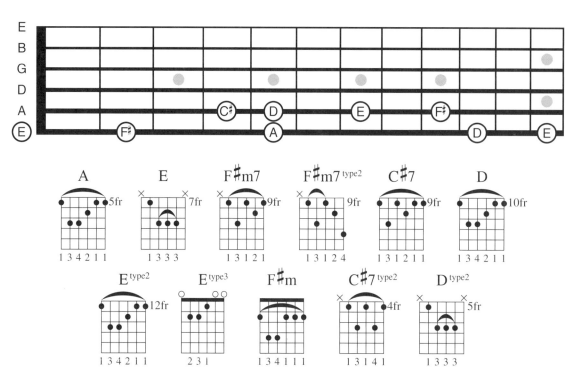

"Hook" presents us with plenty of new challenges, including new chords and sixteenth-note strum patterns. It also makes use of playing the same chord in different spots on the neck. Let's begin with the F#m7 chord. As shown in the chord frames below, the lowered seventh of F# is added to our standard minor form by simply removing our fourth finger. The second type of F#m7 brings the pinky back into the chord but at the twelfth fret. Practice alternating between these two chords:

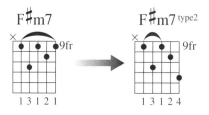

Overall there are five different strum patterns used in "Hook" and they all involve sixteenth notes. When fitting four strums into every beat as sixteenth notes do, the numbers and the "&s" become downstrokes, and the "Es" and "As" become upstrokes. Begin by playing each of these exercises with one chord, which will allow you to focus on the rhythm. When you can do that smoothly, look to the arrangement and add the chord changes to the strum pattern.

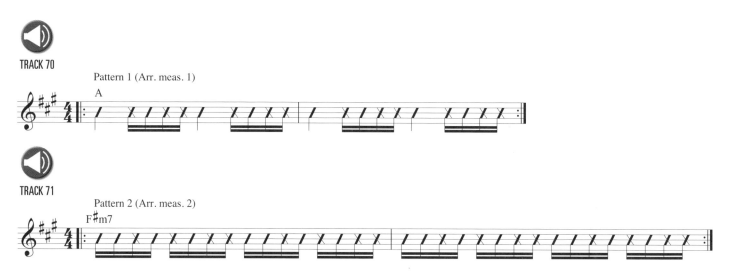

44

"Breakout" – Foo Fighters

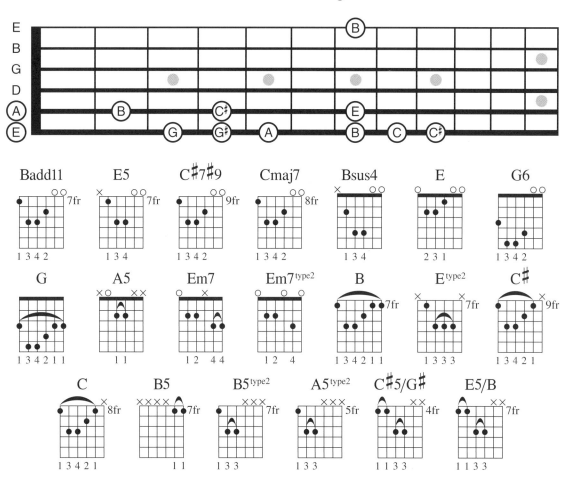

"Breakout" presents many new varieties of barre chords and strumming challenges. To aid in learning the arrangement, let's break it down into smaller pieces and look at some of the new things used in this song.

The first new chord variation that occurs actually removes the barre from our previous chord forms, letting the top two strings ring freely above the chord. You will notice that the rest of the fingering remains the same. Try the following exercise then look to the arrangement and add the strum pattern to the first riff.

The chorus riff of "Breakout" utilizes more standard barre chord forms, with ringing open strings, and introduces Em7. It also incorporates accenting different parts of the chord when you see the accent mark (>). In the following exercise, only strum the top strings of the chord where the accent mark is written. Emphasize the lower notes on the remaining strums. Reference the audio for an example.

TRACK 76

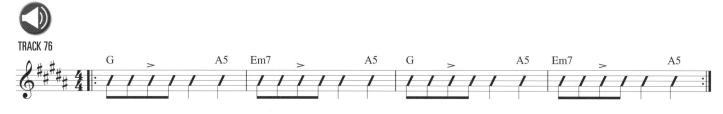

Our next riff introduces the second type of Em7, which actually is not a barre chord. Practice the strumming rhythm slowly while keeping your pick going in the right direction.

TRACK 77

In our next example, the chords from our first riff are played as barre chords without the open strings. The first string is not used, but it won't sound bad if you accidentally strum it on the sixth-string-root chords.

The final riff of the tune uses power chords that utilize the barre. The second two add the fifth below the root for extra girth (i.e., C#5/G# and E5/B). Be careful not to fret any extra notes with your third finger. After completing this exercise, you will have the majority of the arrangement under your fingers.

TRACK 78

TRACK 79

HAL•LEONARD® GUITAR PLAY-ALONG

Complete song lists available online.

This series will help you play your favorite songs quickly and easily. Just follow the tab and listen to the audio to the hear how the guitar should sound, and then play along using the separate backing tracks. Audio files also include software to slow down the tempo without changing pitch. The melody and lyrics are included in the book so that you can sing or simply follow along.

INCLUDES TAB

VOL. 1 – ROCK.................................00699570 / $17.99
VOL. 2 – ACOUSTIC.........................00699569 / $16.99
VOL. 3 – HARD ROCK.......................00699573 / $17.99
VOL. 4 – POP/ROCK.........................00699571 / $16.99
VOL. 5 – THREE CHORD SONGS ....00300985 / $16.99
VOL. 6 – '90S ROCK........................00298615 / $16.99
VOL. 7 – BLUES..............................00699575 / $19.99
VOL. 8 – ROCK...............................00699585 / $16.99
VOL. 9 – EASY ACOUSTIC SONGS ....00151708 / $16.99
VOL. 10 – ACOUSTIC........................00699586 / $16.95
VOL. 11 – EARLY ROCK.....................00699579 / $15.99
VOL. 12 – ROCK POP ....00291724 / $17.99
VOL. 14 – BLUES ROCK.....................00699582 / $16.99
VOL. 15 – R&B...............................00699583 / $17.99
VOL. 16 – JAZZ..............................00699584 / $16.99
VOL. 17 – COUNTRY.........................00699588 / $17.99
VOL. 18 – ACOUSTIC ROCK................00699577 / $15.95
VOL. 20 – ROCKABILLY.....................00699580 / $17.99
VOL. 21 – SANTANA ....00174525 / $17.99
VOL. 22 – CHRISTMAS ....00699600 / $15.99
VOL. 23 – SURF...............................00699635 / $17.99
VOL. 24 – ERIC CLAPTON..................00699649 / $19.99
VOL. 25 – THE BEATLES....................00198265 / $19.99
VOL. 26 – ELVIS PRESLEY..................00699643 / $16.99
VOL. 27 – DAVID LEE ROTH................00699645 / $16.95
VOL. 28 – GREG KOCH......................00699646 / $19.99
VOL. 29 – BOB SEGER.......................00699647 / $16.99
VOL. 30 – KISS...............................00699644 / $17.99
VOL. 32 – THE OFFSPRING..................00699653 / $14.95
VOL. 33 – ACOUSTIC CLASSICS............00699656 / $19.99
VOL. 35 – HAIR METAL......................00699660 / $17.99
VOL. 36 – SOUTHERN ROCK................00699661 / $19.99
VOL. 37 – ACOUSTIC UNPLUGGED ....00699662 / $22.99
VOL. 38 – BLUES.............................00699663 / $17.99
VOL. 39 – '80s METAL.......................00699664 / $17.99
VOL. 40 – INCUBUS..........................00699668 / $17.95
VOL. 41 – ERIC CLAPTON...................00699669 / $17.99
VOL. 42 – COVER BAND HITS...............00211597 / $16.99
VOL. 43 – LYNYRD SKYNYRD................00699681 / $22.99
VOL. 44 – JAZZ GREATS.....................00699689 / $19.99
VOL. 45 – TV THEMES.......................00699718 / $14.95
VOL. 46 – MAINSTREAM ROCK.............00699722 / $16.95
VOL. 47 – JIMI HENDRIX SMASH HITS....00699723 / $22.99
VOL. 48 – AEROSMITH CLASSICS...........00699724 / $19.99
VOL. 49 – STEVIE RAY VAUGHAN ....00699725 / $17.99
VOL. 50 – VAN HALEN: 1978-1984........00110269 / $19.99
VOL. 51 – ALTERNATIVE '90s...............00699727 / $14.99
VOL. 52 – FUNK..............................00699728 / $15.99
VOL. 53 – DISCO.............................00699729 / $14.99
VOL. 54 – HEAVY METAL....................00699730 / $17.99
VOL. 55 – POP METAL.......................00699731 / $14.95
VOL. 57 – GUNS 'N' ROSES.................00159922 / $19.99
VOL. 58 – BLINK 182........................00699772 / $17.99
VOL. 59 – CHET ATKINS.....................00702347 / $17.99
VOL. 60 – 3 DOORS DOWN..................00699774 / $14.95
VOL. 62 – CHRISTMAS CAROLS............00699798 / $12.95
VOL. 63 – CREEDENCE CLEARWATER
            REVIVAL.........................00699802 / $17.99
VOL. 64 – ULTIMATE OZZY OSBOURNE...00699803 / $19.99
VOL. 66 – THE ROLLING STONES...........00699807 / $19.99
VOL. 67 – BLACK SABBATH..................00699808 / $17.99
VOL. 68 – PINK FLOYD –
            DARK SIDE OF THE MOON ...00699809 / $17.99
VOL. 71 – CHRISTIAN ROCK................00699824 / $14.95

VOL. 74 – SIMPLE STRUMMING SONGS..00151706 / $19.99
VOL. 75 – TOM PETTY ....00699882 / $19.99
VOL. 76 – COUNTRY HITS...................00699884 / $16.99
VOL. 77 – BLUEGRASS ....00699910 / $17.99
VOL. 78 – NIRVANA..........................00700132 / $17.99
VOL. 79 – NEIL YOUNG......................00700133 / $24.99
VOL. 81 – ROCK ANTHOLOGY..............00700176 / $22.99
VOL. 82 – EASY ROCK SONGS..............00700177 / $17.99
VOL. 83 – SUBLIME..........................00369114 / $17.99
VOL. 84 – STEELY DAN......................00700200 / $19.99
VOL. 85 – THE POLICE.......................00700269 / $17.99
VOL. 86 – BOSTON...........................00700465 / $19.99
VOL. 87 – ACOUSTIC WOMEN..............00700763 / $14.99
VOL. 88 – GRUNGE...........................00700467 / $16.99
VOL. 89 – REGGAE...........................00700468 / $15.99
VOL. 90 – CLASSICAL POP ....00700469 / $14.99
VOL. 91 – BLUES INSTRUMENTALS ......00700505 / $19.99
VOL. 92 – EARLY ROCK
            INSTRUMENTALS.................00700506 / $17.99
VOL. 93 – ROCK INSTRUMENTALS.........00700507 / $17.99
VOL. 94 – SLOW BLUES......................00700508 / $16.99
VOL. 95 – BLUES CLASSICS.................00700509 / $15.99
VOL. 96 – BEST COUNTRY HITS ....00211615 / $16.99
VOL. 97 – CHRISTMAS CLASSICS..........00236542 / $14.99
VOL. 99 – ZZ TOP............................00700762 / $17.99
VOL. 100 – B.B. KING........................00700466 / $16.99
VOL. 101 – SONGS FOR BEGINNERS .....00701917 / $14.99
VOL. 102 – CLASSIC PUNK..................00700769 / $14.99
VOL. 104 – DUANE ALLMAN................00700846 / $22.99
VOL. 105 – LATIN............................00700939 / $16.99
VOL. 106 – WEEZER.........................00700958 / $17.99
VOL. 107 – CREAM...........................00701069 / $17.99
VOL. 108 – THE WHO........................00701053 / $17.99
VOL. 109 – STEVE MILLER..................00701054 / $19.99
VOL. 110 – SLIDE GUITAR HITS.............00701055 / $17.99
VOL. 111 – JOHN MELLENCAMP............00701056 / $14.99
VOL. 112 – QUEEN...........................00701052 / $16.99
VOL. 113 – JIM CROCE......................00701058 / $19.99
VOL. 114 – BON JOVI........................00701060 / $17.99
VOL. 115 – JOHNNY CASH...................00701070 / $17.99
VOL. 116 – THE VENTURES..................00701124 / $17.99
VOL. 117 – BRAD PAISLEY..................00701224 / $16.99
VOL. 118 – ERIC JOHNSON..................00701353 / $19.99
VOL. 119 – AC/DC CLASSICS................00701356 / $19.99
VOL. 120 – PROGRESSIVE ROCK............00701457 / $14.99
VOL. 121 – U2...............................00701508 / $17.99
VOL. 122 – CROSBY, STILLS & NASH ....00701610 / $16.99
VOL. 123 – LENNON & McCARTNEY
            ACOUSTIC.......................00701614 / $16.99
VOL. 124 – SMOOTH JAZZ..................00200664 / $17.99
VOL. 125 – JEFF BECK.......................00701687 / $19.99
VOL. 126 – BOB MARLEY....................00701701 / $17.99
VOL. 127 – 1970s ROCK.....................00701739 / $17.99
VOL. 129 – MEGADETH.....................00701741 / $17.99
VOL. 130 – IRON MAIDEN...................00701742 / $17.99
VOL. 131 – 1990s ROCK.....................00701743 / $14.99
VOL. 132 – COUNTRY ROCK................00701757 / $15.99
VOL. 133 – TAYLOR SWIFT..................00701894 / $16.99
VOL. 135 – MINOR BLUES ....00151350 / $17.99
VOL. 136 – GUITAR THEMES................00701922 / $14.99
VOL. 137 – IRISH TUNES....................00701966 / $17.99
VOL. 138 – BLUEGRASS CLASSICS.........00701967 / $17.99

VOL. 139 – GARY MOORE ....00702370 / $17.99
VOL. 140 – MORE STEVIE RAY VAUGHAN .00702396 / $24.99
VOL. 141 – ACOUSTIC HITS.................00702401 / $16.99
VOL. 142 – GEORGE HARRISON............00237697 / $17.99
VOL. 143 – SLASH............................00702425 / $19.99
VOL. 144 – DJANGO REINHARDT ....00702531 / $17.99
VOL. 145 – DEF LEPPARD...................00702532 / $19.99
VOL. 146 – ROBERT JOHNSON.............00702533 / $16.99
VOL. 147 – SIMON & GARFUNKEL.........14041591 / $19.99
VOL. 148 – BOB DYLAN.....................14041592 / $17.99
VOL. 149 – AC/DC HITS.....................14041593 / $19.99
VOL. 150 – ZAKK WYLDE....................02501717 / $19.99
VOL. 151 – J.S. BACH........................02501730 / $16.99
VOL. 152 – JOE BONAMASSA..............02501751 / $24.99
VOL. 153 – RED HOT CHILI PEPPERS....00702990 / $22.99
VOL. 155 – ERIC CLAPTON UNPLUGGED.00703085 / $17.99
VOL. 156 – SLAYER..........................00703770 / $19.99
VOL. 157 – FLEETWOOD MAC..............00101382 / $17.99
VOL. 159 – WES MONTGOMERY.............00102593 / $22.99
VOL. 160 – T-BONE WALKER................00102641/ $17.99
VOL. 161 – THE EAGLES ACOUSTIC........00102659 / $19.99
VOL. 162 – THE EAGLES HITS...............00102667 / $19.99
VOL. 163 – PANTERA ....00103036 / $19.99
VOL. 164 – VAN HALEN: 1986-1995.....00110270 / $19.99
VOL. 165 – GREEN DAY......................00210343 / $17.99
VOL. 166 – MODERN BLUES................00700764 / $16.99
VOL. 167 – DREAM THEATER..............00111938 / $24.99
VOL. 168 – KISS.............................00113421 / $17.99
VOL. 169 – TAYLOR SWIFT..................00115982 / $16.99
VOL. 170 – THREE DAYS GRACE............00117337 / $16.99
VOL. 171 – JAMES BROWN...................00117420 / $16.99
VOL. 172 – THE DOOBIE BROTHERS .....00119670 / $17.99
VOL. 173 – TRANS-SIBERIAN
            ORCHESTRA......................00119907 / $19.99
VOL. 174 – SCORPIONS......................00122119 / $19.99
VOL. 175 – MICHAEL SCHENKER...........00122127 / $19.99
VOL. 176 – BLUES BREAKERS WITH JOHN
            MAYALL & ERIC CLAPTON.......00122132 / $19.99
VOL. 177 – ALBERT KING....................00123271 / $17.99
VOL. 178 – JASON MRAZ....................00124165 / $17.99
VOL. 179 – RAMONES........................00127073 / $17.99
VOL. 180 – BRUNO MARS....................00129706 / $16.99
VOL. 181 – JACK JOHNSON.................00129854 / $16.99
VOL. 182 – SOUNDGARDEN.................00138161 / $17.99
VOL. 183 – BUDDY GUY.....................00138240 / $17.99
VOL. 184 – KENNY WAYNE SHEPHERD...00138258 / $17.99
VOL. 185 – JOE SATRIANI...................00139457 / $19.99
VOL. 186 – GRATEFUL DEAD................00139459 / $17.99
VOL. 187 – JOHN DENVER...................00140839 / $19.99
VOL. 188 – MÖTLEY CRÜE...................00141145 / $19.99
VOL. 189 – JOHN MAYER....................00144350 / $19.99
VOL. 190 – DEEP PURPLE...................00146152 / $19.99
VOL. 191 – PINK FLOYD CLASSICS ....00146164 / $17.99
VOL. 192 – JUDAS PRIEST...................00151352 / $19.99
VOL. 193 – STEVE VAI.......................00156028 / $19.99
VOL. 194 – PEARL JAM ....00157925 / $17.99
VOL. 195 – METALLICA: 1983-1988.......00234291 / $22.99
VOL. 196 – METALLICA: 1991-2016.......00234292 / $19.99

Prices, contents, and availability subject to change without notice.

www.halleonard.com

0822
173